2016
CUMULATIVE
SUPPLEMENT

# Pennsylvania Fiduciary Guide



*by*

RICHARD L. GROSSMAN

*and*

JAMES L. HOLLINGER

*Members of the Montgomery County Bar*

GEORGE T. BISEL COMPANY, INC.

710 S. WASHINGTON SQUARE

PHILADELPHIA PENNSYLVANIA

www.bisel.com

Printed in United States of America

Library of Congress Control Number: 2007941856

ISBN: 0-9755281-8-1

**HOW TO USE**

**First refer to main text, then check this supplement using the same reference numbers. Sections added subsequent to publication of the main text, if any, will be included in a supplemental table of contents in this pamphlet.**

**ALWAYS VERIFY CITATIONS BY CONSULTING THE OFFICIAL COURT DECISIONS, RULES, REGULATIONS AND STATUTES**

**If you have any questions, please call us at 800-247-3526. Contact the Bisel Editorial Department directly with your questions and suggestions at tonyd@bisel.com.**

# SUPPLEMENTAL TABLE OF CONTENTS

SUPPLEMENTAL TABLE OF CONTENTS

# SUPPLEMENTAL TABLE OF CONTENTS

## Chapter 1

# STEPS PRELIMINARY TO PROBATE AND GRANT OF LETTERS

---

## § 1.3 FUNERAL AND BURIAL

Act 45 of 2013, signed July 2 and effective in 60 days, amends PEF 305 to deal with the right to control final disposition of the remains of a member of The Armed Forces.

Petitioner alleged he was biological child of decedent, entitled to an intestate share, and asked for order to exhume decedent's body for genetic testing to prove his claim. It was held: Exhumation ordered. *Fox Est.* (O.C. Div. Luzerne), 4 Fiduc. Rep. 3d 380, annot. *Fiduc. Rev.*, Nov. 2014, p. 3.

## § 1.5 EMPLOYMENT OF LEGAL COUNSEL

Attorney who prepared will and administered Crummey trust until discharged in 2008 and his firm could not represent co-executor who petitioned for accounting by agents who transferred testator's funds to joint account with wife. Then the funds were allegedly loaned to the agents. Attorney and firm were disqualified. *Whitly Est.* (O.C. Div. Montg.), 4 Fiduc. Rep. 3d 133, annot. *Fiduc. Rev.*, July 2014, p. 3.

Non-attorney administrator of estate may not proceed to litigate judicial tax sale matter without counsel. *Rowley Est.* (Comm. Ct.), 4 Fiduc. Rep. 3d 249.

Fee agreement between attorney and administrator reserved right . . . "to terminate if you insist upon pursuing or . . . engage in a course of conduct that we consider repugnant or imprudent or with which we have a fundamental disagreement."

After client wrote ex parte communication to court, attorney filed motion to withdraw, which was denied. On appeal, Superior Court reversed. *Bortz Est.*, Pa. Super., May 27, 2015, No. 1428 MDA 2014 (Non-precedential Decision), annot. *Fiduc. Rev.*, Oct. 2015, p. 4.

Chapter 2

# DISPOSITION OF ESTATES INDEPENDENT OF LETTERS

---

## § 2.1 IN GENERAL

Act 35 of 2013, which was effective 60 days after signing by the Governor on July 2, 2013, as to decedents dying on or after the effective date, amends PEF 3102 and PEF 3531 to increase the amount of the estate eligible for distribution under those provisions from $25,000 to $50,000. See annotation in *Fiduciary Review*, Aug. 2013, p. 1.

## § 2.2 PROPERTY AND CLAIMS WHICH MAY PASS WITHOUT ADMINISTRATION

Act 35 of 2013, signed July 2, 2013, and effective in 60 days amends PEF 3101 to increase the amount of deposit accounts which shall, and patient care accounts which may, be paid independent of letters testamentary or of administration from $3,500 to $10,000.

## § 2.4 STATUTORY PROCEDURE FOR PERSONAL ESTATE OF $50,000 OR LESS

Act 35 of 2013, which was effective 60 days after signing by the Governor on July 2, 2013, as to decedents dying on or after the effective date, amends PEF 3102 and PEF 3531 to increase the amount of the estate eligible for distribution under those provisions from $25,000 to $50,000. See annotation in *Fiduciary Review*, Aug. 2013, p. 1.

## Chapter 3

# THE GRANT OF LETTERS OF ADMINISTRATION

---

## § 3.3 FACTS OF DEATH OR PRESUMED DEATH

Presumption of death from exposure to specific peril less than seven years earlier refused. *Goodyear Trust* (O.C. Div. Franklin), 4 Fiduc. Rep. 3d 171.

## § 3.10 BOND REQUIRED—CHANGING THE AMOUNT THEREOF

Register of Wills is not immune from liability under Tort Claims Act for issuance of letters of administration without security; remanded to Orphans' Court for further proceedings to develop factual record, vis-à-vis PEF 3172, as to whether Register "in good faith reasonably believed the conduct was authorized or required by law." *Dorsey v. Redman*, 96 A.3d 332.

Chapter 4

# PROBATE OF WILLS

---

## § 4.3 PRODUCTION OF WILLS AND RELATED DOCUMENTS

Undated will was probated November 6, 2012. A "petition" was filed to "invalidate" the undated will and vacate appointment of administratrix, claiming "generally that there is a 'later' 1991 will" but not producing it. It was held: Petition denied. *Williams Est.* (O.C. Div. Phila.), 4 Fiduc. Rep. 3d 344 annot. *Fiduc. Rev.*, Oct. 2014, p. 1.

## § 4.4 DOCUMENTS WHICH CONSTITUTE A WILL

(2) Handwritten document was testamentary, and thus could be a valid codicil, even though there were some indicia that a future document was contemplated. Matter remanded to orphans' court to hear extrinsic evidence of testatrix' intent. *Tyler Est.* (Pa. Super.), 80 A.3d 797.

## § 4.7 WHERE WILL MUST BE PROBATED

Appeal from probate on ground of lack of jurisdiction, because decedent's domicile was alleged to be Florida, denied: *Perelman Est.*, 3 Fiduc. Rep. 3d 307.

Decedent died at daughter's home in New Jersey. His will was probated, by that daughter as executrix, in Philadelphia.

Son filed "Petition to Revoke Letters," alleging decedent was not domiciled in Pennsylvania at his death.

Court held: Decedent was domiciled in Philadelphia. *Rothberg Est.* (O.C. Div. Phila.), 4 Fiduc. Rep. 3d 403, annot. *Fiduc. Rev.*, Feb. 2015, p. 1.

## § 4.11 DECREE OF PROBATE

Petition to "invalidate" undated probated will, on allegation of existence of later will which is not produced, is "denied without prejudice until such time as a later will has been located and presented for review." A person asserting existence of a later will has the burden of proving that such will was properly executed, more recently than the challenged will. If this burden is met, the Orphans' Court then remands the matter to the Register to determine whether the after-discovered will should be probated. *Williams Est.* (O.C. Div. Phila.), 4 Fiduc. Rep. 3d 344.

Chapter 5

# THE GRANT OF LETTERS TESTAMENTARY

## § 5.4 BOND

Several heirs filed petition for removal of executor, alleging mismanagement and failure to perform duties. They also contended that executor was a nonresident who should be required to post a surety bond.

HELD: Mismanagement not proven, and executor is a resident of Pennsylvania so no bond is required. *Mutchler Est.* (O.C. Div. Monroe), 4 Fiduc. Rep. 3d 107, annot. *Fiduc. Rev.*, Apr. 2014, p. 3.

## § 5.7 REMOVAL OR DEATH OF EXECUTOR

Dual role of executrix/trustee in estates and trusts of both settlor and settlor's wife did not constitute conflict requiring removal. *Estate of Mumma*, 41 A.3d 41 (Pa. Super).

Will named bank, son and grandson as trustees, Grandson and bank are surviving trustees, son having died. Bank petitioned to remove grandson for failure to cooperate. Grandson countered that he had authority to remove the corporate trustee which he claimed he exercised. Bank's motion for partial summary judgment is denied. The dispute will continue with further proceedings. *Lukens Trust* (O.C. Div. Montg.), 3 *Fiduc. Rev.* 3d 113, annot. *Fiduc. Rev.*, May 2013, p. 3.

Removal of trustee under PEF 7766(b)(4) requires petitioner to "show by clear and convincing evidence that: (1) the removal serves the beneficiaries' best interests; (2) the removal is not inconsistent with a material purpose of the trust; (3) a suitable successor trustee is available; and

(4) a substantial change in circumstances has occurred." Petition granted where "approximately six corporate mergers [have led] to entirely different bank officers involved in administering the trusts . . ." which ". . . represents a change of circumstances substantial enough to come within the nofault statutory provisions:" ". . . courts should consider the following factors when determining whether a current trustee or a proposed successor trustee best serves the interests of the beneficiaries: personalization of services; cost of administration; convenience to the beneficiaries; efficiency of service; personal knowledge of trusts' and beneficiaries financial situations; location of trustee as it affects trust income tax; experience; qualifications; personal relationship with beneficiaries; settlor's intent as expressed in the trust document; and any other material circumstances, No one factor in this nonexhaustive list will outweigh the others. Rather, the trial court is to consider these factors if the parties present evidence thereof, on a case-by-case basis," *McKinney Trust* (Pa. Super.), 67 A.3d 824, reversing 1 Fiduc. Rep. 3d 165, annotated in *Fiduciary Review*, April 2012. See annotation in *Fiduciary Review*, July 2013, p. 1.

Decedent's two sons removed as co-executors and as co-trustees for benefit of decedent's wife and temporary substitute appointed to serve. *Martelli Est.* (O.C. Div. Phila.), 8 Fiduc. Rep. 3d 15.

Will named daughter Marlene as executrix, but if she were "unable or unwilling to serve," named replacements seriatim as daughter Marjorie, or daughter Linda, or trust company. Daughter Mary was not named as possible successor.

Marlene obtained letters testamentary, but was removed after hearing establishing conflicts of interest, and Mary and Linda were appointed co-executrices.

On appeal, Superior Court affirmed removal of Marlene, upheld failure to select Marjorie as next in line (she being "aligned with" Marlene). But appointment of Mary and Linda was improper; Linda is appointed sole executrix. *Andrews Est.* (Pa. Super.), 92 A.3d 1226 annot. *Fiduc. Rev.*, Aug. 2014, p. 4.

# Chapter 6

# DUTIES FOLLOWING GRANT OF LETTERS

---

## § 6.1 INTRODUCTION

Executor-son failed to perform properly duties relating to estate administration, resulting in a significant surcharge. This case is a good primer of what an executor should not do. *Grimble Estate* (O.C. Div. Washington), 3 Fiduc. Rep. 3d 224.

Orphans' Court has power to review and correct its own decree; executor not entitled to charge estate fees for counsel retained to prevent his removal. *Rappaport Estate* (O.C. Div. Bucks), 3 Fiduc. Rep. 3d 115.

## § 6.9 BANK ACCOUNTS

Proceeds of $40,000 treasury bill deposited into "in trust for" account belonged to estate and not to daughter named on the account; co-executor proved by clear and convincing evidence that father had planned that all of his assets be divided into three equal shares. *Estate of Strahsmeier* (Pa. Super.), 54 A.3d 359.

Four months before death, decedent removed funds which he had deposited from entireties account and placed them in account in his name alone. No gift was intended and decedent's ownership remained during his lifetime. Funds belong to decedent and pass by terms of his will. *Fawley Est.* (O.C. Div. Chester), 3 Fiduc. Rep. 3d 254, annot. *Fiduc. Rev.*, Sept. 2013, p. 4.

Act 35 of 2013, signed July 2 and effective in 60 days amends PEF 3101 to increase the amount of deposit accounts which shall, and patient care accounts which may, be paid independent of letters testamentary or of administration from $3,500 to $10,000.

Bank account in joint names of decedent and her daughter as joint owners with rights of survivorship at death of mother belongs to daughter.

Executor directed daughter to transfer funds from joint account to estate account and court determined no gift to estate was intended. *Boyce Est.*, 4 Fiduc. Rep. 3d 193.

Joint savings accounts and certificates of deposit in Cayman Islands pass to surviving spouse under PEF 6304. Accounts which existed prior to execution of the agreement were not included in its listing of "separate property," as to which she waived any rights, so the PEF Code provision applies. Accounts created after execution of the agreement belong to survivor because agreement so provided as to such joint assets established by "mutual agreement"; such requisite is clear (even in the absence of the usual signature card in this case) because funds to establish the joint asset were transferred by decedent from an existing joint asset to the new account. *Hornburg Est.*, Pa. Super., No. 1084 WDA 2014 (August 4, 2015). Nonprecedential decision.

## § 6.10 LIFE INSURANCE AND DEATH BENEFITS—SOCIAL SECURITY—MEDICARE—VETERANS' BENEFITS—PENSION BENEFITS

Dispute between decedent's former same-sex domestic partner and decedent's family over proceeds, which involved a history of beneficiary designations by paper and by computer, involved "genuine issue of material fact" rendering summary judgment inappropriate. Insurer did not breach its fiduciary duty under ERISA by filing interpleader, rather than paying alleged primary beneficiary, in light of competing claims. *Gallagher Est.*, Pa. Super., No. 1125 EDA 2014 (7/23/15). Nonprecedential decision (Memorandum by Gantman, P.J.).

## § 6.19 PARTNERSHIP INTERESTS

Estate included minority interests in closely-held corporations. Executors' valuation was challenged in objections to account.

HELD: Valuations were "reasonable and proper." Objections denied, account confirmed. *Bittner Est.* (O.C. Div. Bedford), 5 Fiduc. Rep. 3d 242, annot. *Fiduc. Rev.*, Oct. 2015, p. 3.

## § 6.27 COMPENSATION OF THE PERSONAL REPRESENTATIVE AND ATTORNEY

Decedent's will gave his estate in equal shares to his four children, two of whom were designated as co-executors. Five days before his death, decedent, without telling his other children, transferred the family farm to the son who lived with decedent. The account showed a gross estate of $48,516.61 and total executors' commission of $8,696. The son who received the farm objected and sought to limit the total commission to $2,425,83. The accountants-executors had filed a civil suit against the objectant seeking to set aside the lifetime transfer of the farm. The court which tried that matter ruled in favor of the objectant-son. The Orphans' Court rejected the objectant's position that 5% of the gross estate was the maximum commission allowable under *Johnson Estate*, 4 Fiduc. Rep. 2d 6, and awarded total commissions of 10% of the gross estate. *Duhovis Estate* (O.C. Div. Montg.), 2 Fiduc. Rep. 3d 431, annot. *Fiduc. Rev.*, Dec. 2012, p. 3.

Discussion of dilatory, obdurate, vexatious, arbitrary and bad faith in assessing counsel fees as taxable costs. *Keslar Trust* (O.C. Div. Montg.), 3 Fiduc. Rep. 3d 59.

Decedent's children sought to contest will by challenges to final account; appeal dismissed. Appeal from probate exclusive method to contest will. Orphans' Court also correct in awarding additional counsel fees for defending against the appeal. *Estate of Whitley* (Pa. Super.), 50 A.3d 203.

Trustees successfully defended surcharge action brought by two of three beneficiaries. Issue then arose as to charging of part of the defense expenses against the share of the beneficiary who did not pursue the surcharge. Litigation costs incurred in successful defense by trustee are, in the circumstances, to be borne by the trust as a whole and not apportioned solely to two beneficiaries who initiated the surcharge actions. *McFadden Trusts*, (O.C. Div. Phila.), 3 Fiduc. Rep. 3d 209, annot. *Fiduc. Rev.*, Sept. 2013, p. 1.

Legal fees of executor defending petition for his removal are not payable by estate, where the alleged improprieties concerned "his actions as an agent under decedent's power of attorney during her lifetime." *Estate of Fisher* (Pa. Super.), 83 A.3d 1066. Non-precedential decision.

Administrator of estate, who was scrivener of will, surcharged and removed. "The respondent took commissions totaling $50,470 without having earned one dime. He breached his duty as a personal representative in virtually every way imaginable." *Smick Est.* (O.C. Div. Montg.), 4 Fiduc. Rep. 3d 481.

Executrix claimed fee of $61,282.72, being 6% of gross value of the estate. The *Johnson Estate* schedule would support fee of $29,987.21. Court found neither extraordinary services, nor lack of time and effort or dilatory or bad faith actions, to be involved, which might justify departing from that fee schedule. *Haffner Est.* (O.C. Div. Monroe), 5 Fiduc. Rep. 3d 195.

Compensation of executors approved, despite objections by Attorney General for charitable beneficiaries. Fees ($246,579 in estate of $8 million) were based on a sliding schedule which was "almost invariably used by [decedent] while he was a practicing probate attorney." No time record was kept but the duties performed were "exhaustively outlined" in the "well-reasoned decision" of the orphans' court. *Peters Est.*, Pa. Super., #1359 MDA 2014 (6/17/15) Non-precedential decision.

## § 6.29 MISCELLANEOUS

See annotation concerning Digital Assets: *Fiduc. Rev.*, March 2015, p. 4.

## Chapter 7

# FAMILY EXEMPTION

---

## § 7.2 PERSONS ENTITLED TO THE EXEMPTION

Son lived in household with parents for 56 years before mother's death, excepting only for his absence from 1979 to 1984. Mother suffered stroke in 2006, and after hospital stay she lived in nursing home until her death in 2008. Son claimed family exemption. Son is entitled to family exemption under PEF 3121. *Torkos Estate* (O.C. Div. Northampton), 2 Fiduc. Rep. 3d 127, annot. *Fiduc. Rev.*, Nov. 2012, p. 3.

Chapter 8

# ELECTIVE SHARE OF SURVIVING SPOUSE

---

## § 8.3 EVIDENCE

Plaintiff brought divorce action. Defendant counterclaimed, denying existence of alleged common law marriage and requested declaratory relief under 23 Pa. C.S. 3306. Divorce action dismissed because no marriage existed. *Rotundo v. Jones* (O.C. Div. Berks), 4 Fiduc. Rep. 3d, 139, annot. *Fiduc. Rev.*, June 2014, p. 4.

## § 8.4 EFFECT OF DIVORCE

Beneficiary designation in favor of former spouse is revoked by PEF Code 6111.2 despite fact that the life insurance policy was purchased prior to enactment of that statutory provision. It is the date of the beneficiary designation, not purchase of the policy, which is relevant and because beneficiary designation was made after PEF 6111.2 was enacted there is no issue of retroactive application in this case. See *Parsonese v. Midland Nat'l Ins. Co.*, 706 A.2d 814; *Estate of Hoffman*, 54 A 3d 903; *Lutz v. Monumental Life Ins, Co.*, Pa. Super., (5/4/15) No. 1400 MDA 2014 (Non-precedential decision, aff'g C.P. Lebanon), annot. *Fiduc. Rev.*, July 2015, p. 3.

## § 8.5 SAME SEX MARRIAGE

The title for this section has been changed to SAME SEX MARRIAGE in place of LIVE-IN PARTNER.

The August 29 edition of "I.R.S. Newswire" in I.R. 2013-72 stated the recognition of same sex marriages for federal tax purposes including income and gift and estate taxes. Any same sex marriage legally entered into is covered by this ruling. However, the ruling does not apply to registered domestic partnerships, civil unions or similar formal relationships recognized under state law. See a copy of the I.R.S. ruling and an annotation in *Fiduciary Review*, Oct. 2013, p. 1.

Internal Revenue Service Notice 2014–19, dated April 14, 2014, applies the rule of *U.S. v. Windsor*, 570 U.S. ___ 133 S. Ct. 2675 and *Revenue Ruling* 2013–17 (recognizing, for federal tax purposes, parties to lawful same-sex marriage as spouses) to qualified retirement plans as there described in a series of questions and answers.

Several cases in Federal District Courts in Pennsylvania and Pennsylvania Orphans' Courts have dealt with the issue of the definition of marriage. As a result of the decision in *Whitwood v. Wolf* (USDC ED. Pa.), 992 F.Supp. 2d 410 which was not appealed, Pennsylvania has joined much of the country in recognizing same-sex marriages.

Same sex marriage has been recognized for PA inheritance tax purposes in Inheritance Tax Bulletin 2015-01. See annotation in *Fiduc. Rev.*, May 2013, p. 3.

## § 8.9 DECISIONS UNDER CHAPTER 22

(a) *Property Subject to Election*

Decedent owned "payable on death" Vanguard investment accounts, naming children of prior marriage as beneficiaries.

Spouse elected to take one-third of the accounts pursuant to PEF 2203(a).

It was held: Accounts are subject to election. *Rood Est.* (O.C. Div. Berks). 5 Fiduc. Rep. 3d 15, annot. *Fiduc. Rev.*, Jan. 2015, p. 3. Affirmed 8/28/15, Pa. Super., #1648 MDA 2014.

(f) Widow's unsuccessful attack on agreement (and unsuccessful election against will) rendered her liable for estate's attorney fees per terms of agreement. Her conveyance of assets during the dispute was found to be fraudulent under 12 Pa. C.S.A. 5104. *Miller Est.* (O.C. Div. Carbon), 5 Fiduc. Rep. 3d 319.

(g) *Forfeiture*

Widow elected against husband's will; executor petitioned to strike or vacate the election because she allegedly forfeited her right by reason of desertion.

HELD: Widow's departure from husband because of physical abuse was not desertion which would deprive her of elective share. *Rollins Est.* (O.C. Div. Chester), 3 Fiduc. Rep. 3d 448, annot. *Fiduc. Rev.*, Feb. 2014, p. 1.

Chapter 9

# ADMINISTRATION OF REAL ESTATE

---

## § 9.1 IN GENERAL

Administrator could not appear pro se to present petition to vacate judicial sale due to alleged procedural defects. *In re Estate of Rowley* (Pa. Cmwlth.), 84 A.3d 337.

Decedent, a North Carolina resident, died testate; her will was probated and her executor appointed, by the North Carolina Court. Executor brought action in Bucks County to compel return of property, located there, by grantee, on grounds of fraud.

Orphans' Court sustained grantees' preliminary objection on basis of lack of subject matter jurisdiction. Executor appealed.

HELD: Reversed. *Gentry Estate v. Diamond Rock Hill Realty Inc.*, (Pa. Super.), 111 A.3d 194, annot. *Fiduc. Rev.*, April 2015, p. 2.

Equity action by administrator (successor to executor) seeking to impose constructive trust to set aside conveyances made by decedent's agent dismissed for laches. Decedent had sued her agent seeking money damages, not constructive trust; after her death, executor did not pursue the complaint. Trial court did not abuse its discretion by finding existence of prejudicial delay, where witnesses have died and much time has elapsed. *Fulton v. Fulton* (Pa. Super.), 106 A.3d 127.

## § 9.2 POSSESSION

Co-tenants of property (other co-tenant being an estate which "has not been opened", are entitled to possession where individual in possession did not present credible evidence of a right to occupy the property. *Horn Est. v. Richardson* (C.P. Lycoming), #14-02765 (4/23/15).

## § 9.3 CONTRACTS OF DECEDENT

Specific performance order enforcing exercise of option continues despite delay of 8-12 years during which estate remained in possession and purchaser took no action. Doctrines of laches and estoppel do not apply. Optionee was equitable owner and estate held title as trustee for it and had "affirmative duty" to contact equitable owner to determine if the delay meant that it was abandoning benefit of its specific performance judgment. *Frano Est.* (O.C. Div. Clearfield), 5 Fiduc. Rep. 3d 291.

## § 9.5 SALE OR MORTGAGE BY THE PERSONAL REPRESENTATIVE

Executrix of an insolvent estate filed petition for leave to sell decedent's mortgaged real estate for $130,000. She estimated estate's obligations at nearly $200,000 including the mortgage lien of over $117,000. Mortgagee did not respond to the petition, preliminary decree and citation. The court authorized a "judicial sale" under PEF Code § 3353 and "discharged all liens on the real property, so that the property could be transferred with a clear title." The account listed $120,761.69 as proceeds from the sale of the real property and proposed that estate administration costs including executrix' commission, attorneys' and accountant's fees and funeral and medical expenses be paid in full. The mortgagee was treated as an unsecured creditor. On appeal by mortgagee it was.

HELD: After the judicial sale, mortgagee's "lien on the property remained a secured claim" which attached to the sale proceeds. *Landis Estate* (Pa. Super.), 85 A.3d 506, annot. *Fiduc. Rev.*, Feb. 2014, p. 3. Decision at 3 Fiduc. Rep. 3d 183 *reversed.*

Petition for approval of "unusual sales arrangement" approved even though will gave executrix power of sale and she need not have sought court approval. *Snyder Est.* (O.C. Div. Montg.), 5 Fiduc. Rep. 3d 46.

Private sale of real estate (family auction) was conducted under court order, and objections filed upon estate's report to court were dismissed. Failure to appeal to Superior Court within 30 days under Pa. R.A.P. 342 is waiver of objections. *Krasinski Est.* (O.C. Div. Clearfield), 5 Fiduc. Rep. 3d 275.

Public sale, or "private sale not confined to the parties," directed by court where insufficient credible evidence exists to order partition pursuant to Pa.R.C.P. 1560(a). *Cremers Est.* (O.C. Div. Chester), 4 Fiduc. Rep. 3d 484.

(2) Order of trial court enjoining sale by executor of real estate was interlocutory and unappealable. Appellate Procedure Rules 313 and 342 did not authorize such appeal in the circumstances. *Cherry Est.* (Pa. Super.), 111 A.3d 1204.

(3) Will gave real estate to daughter, Pamela, subject to right of friend, Julia, to "occupy it for life, or until she sooner vacates." Executor petitioned court to allow sale because of poor condition of property. Julia objected.

The Court determined that Julia had a personal right to occupy the portion of the property where she lived and denied the petition despite the allegation that continued residence violated local zoning ordinances. *Miller Est.* (O.C. Div. Chester), 5 Fiduc. Rep. 3d 231, annot. *Fiduc. Rev.*, Sept. 2015, p. 1.

## § 9.8 DISTRIBUTION

For an annotation regarding deeds, devises and Marcellus shale rights, see *Fiduciary Review*, May 2013, p. 1 where *J.P. Morgan Chase Bank, Executor of the Estate of Roswell Miller v. Miller Associates, Inc., Roswell C. Miller, Kenneth B. Miller and BLX, Inc.* (Civ. Action Westm.), 3 Fiduc. Rep. 3d 170 is discussed.

## Chapter 10

# DEBTS AND CLAIMS AGAINST THE ESTATE

---

## § 10.1 IN GENERAL

Widow prevailed in claim made, against estate, under terms of prenuptial agreement. She was awarded attorney fees. *Campbell Est.* (No. 2) (O.C. Div. Montg.), 2 Fiduc. Rep. 3d 369, annot. *Fiduc. Rev.*, Oct. 2012, p. 1.

Claim for repayment of loan was "carefully documented . . . with copies of checks" and "buttressed by . . . highly credible testimony" that payments were loans, not gifts. There was no familial relationship refuting expectation of repayment. *Sipos Est.* (O.C. Div. Phila.), 5 *Fiduc. Rep.* 8d 256, annotated in Fiduc. Rev., Sept. 2015, p. 4. See *Fiduciary Review*, March 2015, p. 3; May 2015, p. 1.

## § 10.4 CLAIMS OF THE UNITED STATES

When decedent died intestate in 2009, he owed legal fees to two law firms among other unpaid creditors. The law firms each filed a Petition for Leave to Execute Judgment against decedent's estate. Answers to the Petitions to Execute were filed by the estate administrators and by unpaid creditors, the Commonwealth and the United States. Both law firms sought to "have their judgments given priority over . . . the tax claims of the Commonwealth and the United States." The Court stated the estate was "insolvent for purposes of this decision." And "Petitioners' claims . . . cannot be paid until after the claims of the United States and the Commonwealth." *Lampley Est.* (O.C. Div. Chester County), 2 Fiduc. Rep. 3d 481, annot. *Fiduc. Rev.*, Dec. 2012, p. 4.

## § 10.5 CLAIMS OF THE COUNTY AND COMMONWEALTH

When decedent died intestate in 2009, he owed legal fees to two law firms among other unpaid creditors. The law firms each filed a Petition for Leave to Execute Judgment against decedent's estate. Answers to the Petitions to Execute were filed by the estate administrators and by unpaid creditors, the Commonwealth and the United States. Both law firms sought to "have their judgments given priority over . . . the tax claims of the Commonwealth and the United States." The Court stated the estate was "insolvent for purposes of this decision." "Petitioners' claims . . . cannot be paid until after the claims of the United States and the Commonwealth." *Lampley Est.* (O.C. Div. Chester), 2 Fiduc. Rep. 3d 481, annot. *Fiduc. Rev.*, Dec. 2012, p. 4.

In addition to the form of notice provided in Appendix 12, see Appendix 12A, for a form which may be used to give the required notice by Fax or Email.

## § 10.7 CONTINGENT AND UNMATURED CLAIMS; CLAIMS SUBJECT TO LITIGATION IN OTHER COURTS

Damage claim involving "breach of contract action" against estate dismissed, without prejudice to ability to file complaint in Common Pleas division. *Durham Est.* (O.C. Div. Chester), 4 Fiduc. Rep. 3d 217.

## § 10.9 CLAIMS FOR HOUSEHOLD SERVICES

Decedent's daughter, Lucy, objected to account which failed to pay her for services to decedent. She claimed $22,500 for "extra services" beyond those for which she had been paid. Court held: objections dismissed. *Donnelly Est.* (O.C. Div. Montg.), 4 Fiduc. Rep. 3d 495, annot. *Fiduc. Rev.*, March 2015, p. 3.

Dorothy, a licensed nurse practitioner, provided nursing services to Rose and her husband, starting prior to his death in 1990 and continuing until Rose's death in 2010. She also performed additional non-nursing services for which she was not paid, and for which she submitted a claim to Rose's estate. Residuary estate was given to charities.

Administrator and attorney general opposed her claim. Court held: claim allowed for period not barred by statute of limitations. *Rubenstein Est.* (O.C. Div. Phila.), 5 Fiduc. Rep. 3d 52, annot. *Fiduc. Rev.*, May 2015, p. 1.

## § 10.10 CLAIMS FOR BREACH OF CONTRACT TO MAKE A WILL

Daughter Jane alleged existence of oral contract to make will giving her the family farm in exchange for her promise to continue to live and work there. She did so from 1983 until 2001, when she left. Father died in 2008. Court held: Enforceable agreement existed. Oral contracts entered into prior to January 1, 1993 are recognized by Pennsylvania law. Jane's inability to perform after 2001 was caused by father, not her. *Meyers Est.* (O.C. Div. Montg), 5 Fiduc. Rep. 3rd 107.

## § 10.11 CLAIMS TO SPECIFIC PROPERTY

William "lived with and had a relationship with" Denise. His will gave his entire estate to his daughter. Denise refused to turn over to estate several items of personal property in her possession, one of which was a Rolex watch which she stated had been given to her son prior to William's death.

Court held: Testimony as to alleged gift by son is barred by "Dead Man's Rule," but testimony by Denise is not. *Estate of Jamack v. Reis* (C.P. Lycoming), 4 Fiduc. Rep. 3d. 25, annot. *Fiduc. Rev.*, Mar. 2014, p. 4.

Orphan's Court had mandatory and exclusive jurisdiction over claims involving management of escrowed proceeds of sale of decedent's house, alleged warranty breaches related to estate administration and alleged breaches of duties by administratrix. Thus, trial division lacked authority involving escrowed assets, but should have transferred entire case to Orphans' Court Division. *Ciuccarelli Est.* (Pa. Super.), 81 A.3d 953.

After Supreme Court "conclusively and definitively" established that individual had no standing to contest will, she lacked standing in separate action involving escrowed proceeds of sale of decedent's property which, belonging to the estate, pass under the will in which she has no interest. *Ciuccarelli Est.* (O.C. Div. Phila.), 4 Fiduc. Rep. 3d 335.

## § 10.14 LIMITATIONS UPON CLAIMS

Attempt to amend complaint filed against deceased owner by substituting co-executors of estate failed because the complaint was a nullity. Slip and fall pedestrian should have filed the complaint against estate within one year after decedent's death pursuant to PEF Code § 3383. Failure to transfer deed from property owner to estate was not concealment or fraud. *McClean v. Dierassi* (Pa. Super.), 84 A.3d 1067.

Where agent, who knew of injury to principal, did not investigate or take action prior to expiration of statute of limitations, action is barred. Situation differs from *Miller*, 463 F.3d 266 (CA-3), where no guardian existed who could have acted for disabled victim. Here, the agent "had the same authority as a court-appointed guardian would have to bring a cause of action." *Brogen v. Northern Health Facilities Inc.*, 152 Montg. Co. L. Rep. 85.

## § 10.16 DEAD MAN'S STATUTE

Dead Man's Rule barred named beneficiaries from testifying but estate failed to establish weakened intellect after meeting the first two prongs of the test for shifting the burden to the beneficiaries to show the absence of undue influence. Named beneficiaries received annuity proceeds. *Jackson Nat'l Life Insur. v. John Heyser et al.* (U.S.D.C. E.D. PA), 4 Fiduc. Rep. 3d 29.

William "lived with and had a relationship with" Denise. His will gave his entire estate to his daughter. Denise refused to turn over to estate several items of personal property in her possession, one of which was a Rolex watch which she stated had been given to her son prior to William's death.

It was held: Testimony as to alleged gift by son is barred by "Dead Man's Rule," but testimony by Denise is not. *Estate of Jamack v. Reis* (C.P. Lycoming), 4 Fiduc. Rep. 3d. 25, annot. *Fiduc. Rev.*, Mar. 2014, p. 4.

Chapter 11

# SURVIVAL, ABATEMENT AND CONTROL OF ACTIONS

## § 11.5 STATUTES OF LIMITATIONS

The document at issue was simply a note obligating A to repay R the sum of $15,000 five years from the date of the loan. As such the four year statute of limitations contained in 42 Pa.C.S.A. 5523(a)(7) applied and not the six year limitation under the Uniform Commercial Code, 13 Pa.C.S.A. 3104. *Sovich v. Estate of Sovich* (Pa. Super.), 55 A.3d 1161.

Survival action was dismissed when instituted after statute of limitations expired. There can be "relation back" where a personal representative was appointed after the statute of limitations expired if the personal representative took affirmative steps to be appointed prior thereto. However, here there were no affirmative steps taken to be appointed until after filing the action and after the expiration of the statute of limitations. ". . . the initial . . . writ of summons, which listed only Decedent as plaintiff, was a legal nullity." *DeFranco v. Seneca Foods Corp.* (Pa. Super.), 6/18/14, No. 1900-WDA 2013 (Non-precedential decision), annot. *Fiduc. Rev.*, Nov. 2014, p. 4.

The extension of the statute of limitations provided in PEF 3376 is not applicable to an unliquidated personal injury tort claim since it is not a "debt or liability". *Prevish v. Northwest Medical Center*, 692 A.2d 192. See *Fiduc. Rev.*, Nov. 2014, p. 4.

# Chapter 12

# INVENTORY

---

## § 12.9 ASSETS WHICH SHOULD BE INCLUDED IN INVENTORY: FORM OF INVENTORY ENTRY

Grandfather clock, which is attached to wall by bolts, is not part of real property since it is not essential to use of the residence and remains personalty. *In re Estate of Vance*, 95 Westmoreland 107.

Chapter 13

# PENNSYLVANIA INHERITANCE, ESTATE AND INCOME TAXES

---

## § 13.1 IN GENERAL; TIMETABLE CORRECTION PROCEDURE— WHEN REQUIRED

October/November 2012 issue of "Tax Update" (#164) sets forth procedures for corrections to returns filed.

To report errors such as transposed figures, miscalculations and obvious duplication of assets, an estate must notify the Department of Revenue of the mistake by letter. The letter requesting administrative adjustment must identify the alleged error and the proposed correction. The letter, along with any documentation supporting the adjustment, should be directed to:

PA Department of Revenue
Bureau of Individual Taxes
Post Assessment Review Unit
PO Box 280601
Harrisburg, PA 17128-0601

Questions regarding correcting an error on a filed return may be directed to the Inheritance and Realty Transfer Tax Division at 717-787-8327.

See provisions of new form REV-1500 released on December 17, 2014 by PA Department of Revenue. *Fiduc. Rev.*, Jan. 2015, p. 1.

## § 13.2 NATURE OF THE INHERITANCE TAX AND PERSONS LIABLE

Handwritten will interpreted in declaratory judgment action. Precatory language did not reduce outright gift. Inheritance tax allocated per Section 9144(f) of inheritance tax statute where will did not contain a tax clause and there was no residue. *Heckendorn Est.* (O.C. Div. Cumb.), 5 Fiduc. Rep. 3d 208.

## § 13.5 RATE OF TAX

*Warnock Est.*, 1 Fiduc. Rep. 3d 437 was affirmed by Commonwealth Court under the name *Himmelberger v. Dept. of Revenue*, 47 A. 3d 160.

See *Fiduciary Review*, November 2012, p. 1 for a Department of Revenue commentary concerning newly created agricultural exemptions and discussion of possible issues addressed by the commentary, as well as other issues not resolved.

Failure of Commonwealth to appear at hearing before Common Pleas waived right to raise issue on appeal. The estate asserted that beneficiary was decedent's common law wife entitled to the spousal rate of 0%. *Sheluga Est.* (Cmwlth Ct.), 3 Fiduc. Rep. 3d 181, annot. *Fiduc. Rev.*, May 2013, p. 4.

With the recognition of same-sex marriage, the spousal rate of 0 percent will now be applicable to such couples. *See* § 8.5, *infra*.

## § 13.9 PROPERTY AND TRANSFERS NOT TAXABLE

(7) Same sex marriage has been recognized for PA inheritance tax purposes in Inheritance Tax Bulletin 2015-01. See annotation in *Fiduc. Rev.*, May 2013, p. 3.

(11) *Act No. 52 of 2013 was signed by the Governor on July 9, 2013, and creates a new exemption in estates of decedents dying on and after July 1, 2013. A.* A new Section 9011(t) is enacted, to create an exemption for family business interests transferred to certain family members.

In order to qualify for the exemption, certain tests apply to the "proprietorship" or the "entity" in the "trade or business": net book value less than $5 million, fewer than 50 employees, in existence for five years and, as to an "entity," is wholly owned by decedent and certain family members and the principal purpose of which is not managing its investments. Family ownership must continue for seven years after the death. If the transfer of an interest into an "entity" occurs within one year prior to death, it must have been for a "legitimate business purpose."

Recapture, and reporting, provisions resembling those which apply to the family agricultural exemption (Section 9111(s) and (s.1)—Act 85 of 2012) are included. In addition, "expenses, debts, obligations and liabilities" incurred in connection with the exempted interest are disallowed under new clause (5) of Section 9130.

The new "contemplation of death" provision in Section 9111(t)(2.1) disqualifies property transferred into the business within one year prior to death, unless "for a legitimate business purpose".

There is also the exclusion, in the Section 9111(t)(5) definition of "qualified family-owned business interest," of an entity with the "principal purpose" or "management of investments or income-producing assets" owned by it. See annotation in *Fiduciary Review*, Aug. 2013, p. 1.

## § 13.11 VALUATION, COMPUTATION AND PAYMENT OF TAX

Valuation adopted by executors sustained and sale of shares approved. Agreement was ambiguous so parol testimony was admissible to interpret provision for valuation, *Bittner Est.* (O.C. Div. Bedford), 5 Fiduc. Rep. 3d 242, annot. *Fiduc. Rev.*, Oct. 2015, p. 3.

## § 13.12 ALLOCATION

Intestate decedent's estate subject to inheritance tax included probate assets, IRA accounts and "in trust for" accounts. Administrator paid aggregate inheritance tax from probate estate. Objections to account, filed by intestate heirs, alleged tax on non-probate assets should have been paid by named beneficiaries thereof. Objection sustained, *O'Levich Est.* (O.C. Div. Monroe), 3 Fiduc. Rep. 3d 64, annot. *Fiduc. Rev.*, Apr. 2013, p. 1.

Will directed that all taxes "together with the expenses of my last illness and all administration expenses" shall be "paid out of and charged against my estate." The phrase "together with . . . administration expenses" requires the taxes to be paid prior to allocation and distribution "as that is how the administration expenses are paid." *Davis Est.*, Pa. Super. No. 1347 WDA 2014 (non precedential decision), reversing 5 Fiduc. Rep. 3d 8, which was annotated in Fiduciary Review, March 2015. (By order Sept. 21, 2015, Memorandum Opinion converted to published opinion per "Superior Court Operating Procedure § 64.37 (B)").

## § 13.18 PENNSYLVANIA INCOME TAX

Fiduciary income tax short period returns for years beginning in 2014 on 2014 PA-41 forms available only upon request from Bureau of Individual Taxes Director's office at 717-787-8346 may be filed. Generally, forms for 2014 will be available in January 2015 without special requests. Other changes include withholding required on PA source income distributed or distributable to non-PA residents, a requirement that a fiduciary keep an accurate list of beneficiaries and penalties of $250 each for failure to file PA-41 or Schedules RK-1 or NRK-1. Non-resident estates or trusts with a resident beneficiary are required to file PA-41. Credits for taxes paid to foreign countries are no longer permitted.

Inter vivos trusts "located in, administered in, and governed by the laws of Delaware" without any Pennsylvania income or assets, are not subject to Pa. income tax, even though settlor was a Pennsylvania resident when he created trusts and discretionary beneficiaries are Pennsylvania residents. *McNeal v. Pa.*, Commonwealth Court, 5/24/13. *See* 2014 Pa. 41: Instructions for requirement to file Pa. return if nonresident estate or trust had Pa. beneficiary.

## § 13.19 TAX AND RENT REBATE

Estate of person who paid property taxes, and was otherwise eligible for a rebate under the Senior Citizens Property Tax and Rent Rebate Assistance Act, but who died after the payment but before December 31 of the claim year, is entitled to the rebate. *Muscarella, Executor of Carbo Estate v. Comm. of Pa.* (Pa. Commonwealth Court), 87 A.3d 966.

## Chapter 14

# FEDERAL ESTATE AND INCOME TAXES

---

## § 14.1 NATURE OF TAX AND PERSONS LIABLE

The August 29 edition of "I.R.S. Newswire" in I.R. 2013-72 stated the recognition of same sex marriages for federal tax purposes including income and gift and estate taxes. Any same sex marriage legally entered into is covered by this ruling. However, the ruling does not apply to registered domestic partnerships, civil unions or similar formal relationships recognized under state law. See a copy of the I.R.S. ruling and an annotation in *Fiduciary Review*, Oct. 2013, p. 1. See § 8.5 for Pennsylvania recognition of same-sex marriage.

## § 14.3 RATE OF TAX

The gift and estate tax rate on amounts in excess of the exclusion amount ($5,340,000 in 2014 $5,430,000 in 2015 and $5,450,000 in 2016) has been increased to 40% for person dying after December 31, 2012 as set forth in the American Taxpayer Relief Act of 2012.

## § 14.5 DEDUCTIONS AND CREDITS

The "American Taxpayer Relief Act of 2012" (ATRA) made permanent the "portability" rule that had been in effect only for 2011 and 2012 decedents. Under that rule, any portion of that applicable exclusion amount ($5.25 million for 2013, $5,340,000 for 2014 and $5,430,000 for 2015) not utilized in an estate could be available to the decedent's surviving spouse in his or her later return. See annotation in *Fiduciary Review*, Mar. 2013, p. 3.

I.R.S. Regulations for electing portability of a predeceased spouse's unused exclusion have been issued. T.D. 9725 (6/16/15).

(1) The exclusion amount for 2013 for federal estate tax purposes is $5,250,000 and for 2014 is $5,340,000 for 2015 is $5,430,000 and for 2016 is $5,450,000. This amount will be adjusted annually in accordance with the American Taxpayer Relief Act of 2012.

In addition, portability provisions previously enacted will continue.

(2)(c) Federal Estate Tax deduction allowed for funds paid to charities in settlement of allegations of undue influence by scrivener/beneficiary/joint owner. The settlement payments resembled the benefits which charities would have received under the will. *I.R.S. Letter Ruling* 201236022, CCH Fed. Est. & Gift Tax Rep. ¶35,787.

Federal Estate Tax charitable deduction not allowed where, at time of filing of return, litigation threat meant that the fund "could not be considered permanently set aside" per I.R.S. 642(c)(2). *Estate of Belmont v. Comm'r*, 144 T.C. #6.

(2)(e) State death taxes will continue to be a deduction for federal estate tax purposes under 2012 legislation.

(3)(a) Since state death taxes continue to be a deduction for federal estate tax purposes, they will not revert to being a credit in years after 2012.

Internal Revenue Service has issued a simplified method for certain taxpayers to obtain an extension of time under § 301.9100-3 of the Procedure and Administration Regulations to make a "portability" election under § 2010(c)(5)(A) of the Internal Revenue Code (Code), by which a decedent's unused exclusion amount (deceased spousal unused exclusion amount, or DSUE amount) becomes available to apply to the surviving spouse's subsequent transfers during life or at death. No user fee is required for submissions filed under this revenue procedure. *Rev. Proc.* 2014–18 (26 CFR 601.201).

## § 14.8 ASSMENT AND APPEAL

I.R.S. has announced that closing letters for returns filed on or after June 1, 2015 will be issued only upon request, which should be made no sooner than four months after filing the return.

## § 14.10 ESTATE'S INCOME TAX

The currently legislated 3.8% additional Medicare tax imposed on taxpayers beginning in 2013 would apply to trusts and estates. The tax is payable on the lesser of (1) undistributed net investment income or (2) the excess of adjusted gross income over the threshold for the highest trust and estate income tax bracket.

Investment income includes dividends, taxable interest, capital gains, annuities, royalties and rental income, reduced by related investment expenses.

In many estates and trusts, investment income other than capital gains would be distributed to the income beneficiaries, so most often the 3.8% additional tax would be payable only where capital gains exceeded the threshold for the highest bracket, which is $11,950 for 2013. *Fiduc. Rev.*, Dec. 2012, p. 4. For 2014, the Threshold is $12,150.

The top bracket for estates and trusts after 2012 will be 39.6 percent and the maximum capital gains and qualified dividends rate will be 20 percent.

I.R.S. has issued final regulations "providing guidance on which costs incurred by estates or trusts other than grantor trusts . . . are subject to the 2 percent floor for miscellaneous itemized deductions under Section 67(a) . . . " Reg. § 1.67-4, 26 CFR Part 1, Federal Register 5/9/14.

# Chapter 15

# ACCOUNTING

---

## § 15.1 DUTY TO ACCOUNT

Named executors renounced nominations and attorney Carroll was appointed administrator dbncta. He filed a petition to compel agent Michael Fein, who had acted for decedent under power of attorney, to file an account of his actions. Such account was filed, and agent also filed a "petition for declaratory relief" requesting that any action against him for alleged breach of duties be ". . . now and forever barred by the statute of limitations . . ."

Court held: Petition denied. *Moskowitz Est.* (O.C. Div. Delaware), 3 Fiduc. Rep. 3d 413, annot. *Fiduc. Rev.*, Dec. 2013, p. 3.

Petition for removal denied, but executor of mother's estate ordered to file account, and to return to estate funds he withdrew as agent under mother's power of attorney prior to her death because the power did not authorize such action. *Coury Estate* (O.C. Div. Carbon), 4 Fiduc. Rep. 3d 436.

## § 15.7 FORM OF ACCOUNTING

Delete word "verification" on page 310 of text.

## § 15.10 OBJECTIONS TO ACCOUNTS—CONFIRMATION OF ACCOUNTS

Will named brother-in-law and testator's wife as co-executors. Wife and testator died in accident, and will authorized law firm to select successor co-executor; it selected associate of firm, who qualified (with testator's brother-in-law who was a partner in the firm) in 1993. Associate left the firm on December 31, 1995; the firm "ceased doing business" in December 1996.

Various proceedings culminated in a "pro forma" account, filed by the heir (the co-executors having failed to file despite numerous orders to do so), showing over $765,000 missing. Judgments entered against co-executors. *Loher Est.* (O.C. Div. Chester), 3 Fiduc. Rep. 3d 71, annot *Fiduc. Rev.*, Apr. 2013, p. 3.

Niece and nephews not identified as beneficiaries or creditors filed petition seeking accounting by attorney-scrivener of deceased uncle's inter vivos trust. Petition denied since they lacked standing. *Frye Trust* (O.C. Div. Phila.), 3 Fiduc. Rep. 3d 251, annot. *Fiduc. Rev.*, Sept. 2013, p. 3.

Executor's records relating to management of the estate ordered to be produced to beneficiaries and a privilege log of documents withheld on the basis of fiduciary privilege was directed. *Thouron Est. (No. 2)* (O.C. Div. Chest.), 3 Fiduc. Rep. 3d 443.

Executor's petition to compel discovery before objections to accounting filed; rule allowing pre-complaint discovery applied. *Robinson Est.* (O.C. Div. Monroe), 4 Fiduc. Rep. 3d 105, annot. *Fiduc. Rev.*, July 2014, p. 4.

In 1995, Fred qualified as executor of mother's estate. He filed his accounting in 2013. Objections were filed by executor of his sister Alice's estate (she died in 2007), essentially complaining of the 18 years it took Fred to "settle" the estate. It was held: Objections dismissed. *Eiswert Est.* (O.C. Div. Lycoming), 4 Fiduc. Rep. 3d 323, annot. *Fiduc. Rev.*, Jan. 2015, p. 1.

Surcharge not justified where approximately 3-year delays in administration of estate and trust were not a breach of duty of fiduciaries and did not cause harm to charitable beneficiaries. Failure to give prompt notice to Attorney General was excusable oversight where notices were given to charitable beneficiaries. *Connor Est.* (O.C. Div. Chester), 4 Fiduc. Rep. 3d 456.

## Chapter 16

# DISTRIBUTION

---

## § 16.1 IN GENERAL

Act 35 of 2013, which is effective 60 days after signing by the Governor on July 2, as to decedents dying on or after the effective date, amends PEF 3102 and PEF 3531 to increase the amount of the estate eligible for distribution under those provisions from $25,000 to $50,000. See annotation in *Fiduciary Review*, Aug, 2013, p. 1.

Beneficiary designation by participant in Public School Employees Retirement System was valid under 24 Pa.C.S. 8507(e) as a "written designation" even though not solely in the retiree's handwriting and corrections in second submission were not initialed. *Snizaski v. Public School Employees' Retirement Board*, Pa. Supreme, 5/28/13.

Beneficiary designation in annuity contract controlled over contrary provision in decedent's later will. He had earlier complied with divorce agreement by designating children of prior marriages as beneficiaries on annuity company form, but later signed a will purporting to designate different beneficiaries. Evenly divided Supreme Court affirmed Superior Court, which had reversed orphans' court award of proceeds under the will; Superior Court applied ". . . longstanding principles on contract and probate law." *Alkhafaji v. TIAA-CREF,* (Pa. 2013), 69 A.3d 219.

## § 16.2 RISK DISTRIBUTION

Two separate distributions were made to beneficiaries prior to filing account. It developed that an overdistribution was made, and the executor was surcharged upon audit of the account. The executor filed a Motion to compel the beneficiaries to reimburse the estate under the terms of the Release which they signed at the time of the risk distribution.

HELD: Motion granted. *Shilling Est.* (O.C. Div. Adams), 4 Fiduc. Rep. 3d 8, annot. *Fiduc. Rev.*, Jan. 2014, p. 1.

Family settlement agreement was valid, despite claim by beneficiary that she was subjected to fraud, duress and undue influence when signing it. She may not have understood the arrangement, claiming "no one told her" the difference between her share under the will and the agreement, but not understanding is not equivalent to being defrauded; she had a copy of the will, but did not retain counsel nor did she carefully review the documents. *Boardman Est.* (Pa. Super.), 80 A.3d 820.

## § 16.3 ENFORCEMENT OF DISTRIBUTION BY CREDITORS AND DISTRIBUTEES

Will created power in widow to appoint principal of marital trust ". . . outright or in trust, to or for any, one or more of my issue . . .". Widow's will expressly appointed principal to separate trusts for benefits of daughter Karyn and son Scott and their issue. Nothing was appointed to daughter Wendy.

Trustee sought declaratory judgement validating the exercise of the power: Wendy opposed it. It was held: Summary judgment granted; widow "properly exercised the power of appointment." *Zucker Est.* (O.C. Div. Montg), 4 Fiduc. Rep. 3d 369, annot. *Fiduc. Rev.*, Oct. 2014, p. 3, aff'd Pa. Super., No. 2727 EDA 2014 (Aug. 5, 2015).

Decedent designated "trustee(s) or successor(s) as provided in last will" as beneficiary of her life insurance policy. The effectiveness of references in her will to insurance was in issue. It was held: Will created trust for receipt of proceeds. *Thomas Will* (O.C. Div. Phila.), 4 Fiduc. Rep. 3d 348, annot. *Fiduc. Rev.*, Dec. 2014, p. 1.

## § 16.5 DETERMINATION OF DISTRIBUTEES

In terrorem clause not enforced where Orphans' Court found that heirs had "probable cause" to litigate.

Their position met the definition of 42 Pa.C.S. § 8352(1) as to "Existence of Probable Cause." See PEF 2521. *Estate of Fisher*, (Pa. Super.), 83 A.3d 1066. Non-precedential decision.

Charitable trust provision lacked details about the particular cause to receive fund and method of distribution. Bequest was therefore awarded outright to charities selected by trustees. *Haffner Est.* (O.C. Div. Monroe), 5 Fiduc. Rep. 3d 195, annot. *Fiduc. Rev.*, Aug. 2015, p. 1.

Exercise of power by donee disposes of assets of the donor so the appointment relates back to the instrument which created the power, as though actually embodied therein. The appointment is read into the will creating it. Therefore, except for the donee's naming of appointees and method of distribution, the other provisions of the donors will remain operative. In this case, the appointment did not of itself create "an entire separate trust document, although [the donee] could have done so" and could also create "complete stand-alone trust instrument" if he wishes. Since he did not do so, administrative provisions in donor's will—including beneficiaries' ability to replace trustee—still apply. *Cassatt Trust* (O.C. Div. Montg.), 5 Fiduc. Rep. 3d 151.

Gift of income to Chestnut Hill Hospital—a non-profit corporation—was in issue because hospital was sold to a for-profit entity. Income awarded to charitable foundation which had been designated, in the Orphans' Court division order approving the sale, to receive the hospital's endowment and similar finds. *Geschick Trust* (O.C. Div. Phila.), 5 Fiduc. Rep. 3d 203.

## § 16.8 INTESTATE DISTRIBUTION

Decedent's sister (and other "possible intestate heirs") alleged that surviving spouse had forfeited her rights in estate by reason of PEF 2106(a). Despite fact that spouses lived separately for almost 30 of their 40 years of marriage, surviving wife did not "desert" her husband, and is entitled to her intestate share. *Bortz Est.* (O.C. Div. Westmoreland), 2 Fiduc. Rep. 3d 342, annot. *Fiduc. Rev.*, Oct. 2012, p. 4.

Testator's will, drafted and executed without advice of counsel, stated that the exclusion of three named children was intentional. However, the failure to provide for distribution of residue created a partial intestacy. The court ruled that the excluded children were included along with two not so excluded—in distribution of the residue. *Zeevering Est.*, (Pa. Super.), 78 A.3d 1106, affirming 3 *Fiduc. Rep.* 3d 51, annot. *Fiduc. Rev.*, Jan. 2013, p. 4.

Divorce was pending but affidavits establishing grounds for divorce had not been filed, so the rights of the surviving spouse remained in place. *McGarrity Est.* (O.C. Div. Chester), 2 Fiduc. Rep. 3d 447.

Under PEF 6111.1 and Divorce Code 3323(g) as applied to the facts of this case, estate of deceased husband was not entitled to bar his widow from receiving husband's share in company's 401(k) profit-sharing plan despite wife's pending divorce action. *McGarrity Est.* (O.C. Div. Chester), 2 Fiduc. Rep. 3d 447.

Under 20 Pa.C.S. 6111.2 the parties must affirmatively indicate in their written contracts that the beneficiary designation shall survive the divorce and in the absence of such wording, the former spouse is to be treated as if she predeceased the decedent where former spouse was named beneficiary after enactment of the above provision. *Estate of Robert D. Hoffman* (Pa. Super), 54 A.3d 903.

Paternity by Estoppel is inapplicable to intestate estate where children of putative father (determined not to be decedent's father by DNA testing) asserted the doctrine and its application would not further the public policy that "children should be secure in knowing who their parents are." *Hooper Est.* (Pa. Super.), 80 A.3d 815.

Executor appealed from Orphans' Court's refusal to find that father of 17 year old decedent had failed to support or had deserted her: It was held: Affirmed; there was no forfeiture. *Fuller Est.* (Pa. Super.), 87 A.3d 330, annot. *Fiduc. Rev.*, Apr. 2014, p. 1.

## § 16.9 SURVIVORS SPOUSE AND PRETERMITTED CHILDREN

Gift to Foundation did not create a trust as to which donor would have standing to force charity to take corporate actions he alleged were basic to his gift. No such conditional gift was established. *Foundation for Anglican Christian Tradition*, Pa. Comm. Ct. #2164 C.D. 2013 (Nov. 5, 2014), 5 Fiduc. Rep. 3d 1, 103 A.3d 425.

## § 16.9A MINORS

Presumption of paternity not applicable where preserving and protecting marriage not implicated, and in any event evidence rebutted any such presumption. *Bostick Trust* (O.C. Div. Montg.), 4 Fiduc. Rep. 3d 241.

Forfeiture by father of right to share in wrongful death and survival action damages arising from minor child's death was enforced under PEF 2106 for willful failure to support for one year prior to the death. Father alleged lack of willfulness because mother "told him Decedent was not his . . . ", so he did not know he had duty to support. However, the ". . . evidence . . . supports the trial court's determination that Evans knew Decedent was his child."

*Stevenson v. Kantor et al.*, Pa. Super., Sept. 26, 2014, #222 EDA 2014 (Non-precedential decision).

## § 16.10 ADOPTEES

Testator died in 1955. His will did not expressly exclude adoptees as issue, and Wills Act of 1947 was applicable. Adopted daughter of an income beneficiary sought inclusion as issue. Objection of another beneficiary contested that status because adoption occurred after testator's death.

It was held: Adoptee can qualify as issue if she can establish a parent-child relationship during minority. *Armistead Trust* (O.C. Div. Del.), 4 Fiduc. Rep. 3d 233, annot. *Fiduc. Rev.*, Sept. 2014, p. 1.

## § 16.22 SLAYERS

Joseph killed his parents and his twin brother. He was found "guilty but mentally ill on three counts of first degree murder." His guardian ad litem contested application of the Slayer's Act to deny Joseph an interest in his mother's estate. It was held: Joseph's intestate interest in his mother's estate is forfeited because he is a "slayer." *McAndrew Est.* (O.C. Div. Montg.), 5 Fiduc. Rep. 3d 43, annot. *Fiduc. Rev.*, Feb. 2015, p. 3.

## § 16.23 DIVORCE

Decedent's wife entitled to receive profit sharing plan survivor benefits rather than decedent's children as named beneficiaries; ERISA trumps PEF Code 6111.2. *Mancilla Est.* (O.C. Div. Chest.), 3 Fiduc. Rep. 3d 297.

Divorce action may be terminated by surviving spouse even though grounds had been established prior to death of other spouse. 23 Pa.C.S. § 3323(d.1) does not mandate equitable distribution on death of a spouse after grounds for divorce have been established; it simply provides the surviving spouse with the option to continue with equitable distribution instead of the divorce action automatically abating upon the death. *Tosi v. Kizis* (Pa. Super.), 85 A.2d 585.

Beneficiary designation in favor of former spouse is revoked by PEF Code 6111.2 despite fact that the life insurance policy was purchased prior to enactment of that statutory provision. It is the date of the beneficiary designation, not purchase of the policy, which is relevant and because beneficiary designation was made after PEF 6111.2 was enacted there is no issue of retroactive application in this case. See *Parsonese v. Midland Nat'l Ins. Co.*, 706 A.2d 814; *Estate of Hoffman*, 54 A.3d 903; *Lutz v. Monumental Life Ins. Co*. Pa. Super. (5/4/15) No. 1400 MDA 2014 (Non-precedential decision, aff'g C.P. Lebanon), annot. *Fiduc. Rev.*, July 2015, p. 3.

## § 16.25 TANGIBLE PERSONAL PROPERTY

Will gave "the Maujer rifle" to brother (Glenn).

Executors filed declaratory judgment action, claiming Glenn should receive only one Mauser rifle; Glenn countered with claim for entire collection of ten "Mauser Rifles." The court held: Glenn is entitled to all ten rifles. *Estate of Wilson Fox v. Glenn Fox, Jr.* (O.C. Div. Somerset), 5 Fiduc. Rep. 3d 181, annot *Fiduc. Rev.*, Aug. 2015, p. 1.

## § 16.26 ADJUDICATION

Will provided that "it is my wish that my daughter and my wife operate said farms [if that] can be profitably done" or if not, that "said farms be sold and the proceeds divided . . ." Property is approximately 600 acres (wooded, tillable, residential rental and small airstrip with hangars) and, for the 43 years since decedent's death has been used for farming, strip mined for coal, timbered and rented for storage. Since estate is not being used for "farming" as commonly defined, ". . . after 43 years, the time to close the estate has come." *Albert Est.* (O.C. Div. Clearfield), 5 Fiduc. Rep. 3d 306.

## § 16.29 DISTRIBUTION BY THE PERSONAL REPRESENTATIVE

Widow is estopped from claim to proceeds of decedent's malpractice action settlement which . . . is at odds with that presented in her petition for the approval of the settlement and allocation of the proceeds . . ." and also with her reporting of the proceeds in the inheritance tax return. *Estates of Neacosia* (O.C. Div. Lehigh), 4 Fiduc. Rep. 3d 1.

## § 16.32 ENFORCEMENT AND CONTROL OF CHARITABLE GIFTS

Distribution of assets of volunteer fire department on revocation of its charter and articles of incorporation. *Guyasuta Volunteer Fire Department* (O.C. Div. Allegh.), 3 Fiduc. Rep. 110.

Decedent died intestate. Foxman Torah Institute filed claim to entire estate, alleging an oral pledge to it (less another pledge, costs and taxes). Administrator filed declaratory judgment action.

HELD: Motion for judgment on pleadings, dismissing claim, granted. *Stein Est.* (O.C. Div. Montg.), 4 Fiduc. Rep. 3d 218, annot. *Fiduc. Rev.*, Sept. 2014, p. 3.

Orphans' Court improperly applied *cy pres* doctrine where hospital would continue its non-profit activities despite changed corporate identity. "Through a series of complicated transactions, Bloomsburg Hospital and ancillary corporate entities have been joined under the larger corporate umbrella of . . ." Geisinger Health System Foundation.

But ". . . there is no evidence that the trust provision has failed" and the funds are being used as settlors' intended. Order that articles of incorporation of Bloomsburg Hospital be amended to assure use of funds locally and not at other locations served by the acquiring hospital system was proper. *In re Shoemaker*, Pa. Super., 828 MDA 2014, May 7, 2015.

Surcharge not justified where approximately 3 year delays in administration of estate and trust were not a breach of duty of fiduciaries and did not cause harm to charitable beneficiaries. Failure to give prompt notice to Attorney General was excusable oversight where notices were given to charitable beneficiaries. *Connor Est.* (O.C. Div. Chester), 4 Fiduc. Rep. 3d 456.

## § 16.37 POWER OF ATTORNEY GIFTS

Agent under decedent's power of attorney had no power to gift the decedent's annuity to himself under PEF 5601.2(c). Proceeds of the annuity is a non-probate asset in the form of an annuity and belongs to the agent as an individual as designated beneficiary of the annuity proceeds. *McCauley Est.* (O.C. Div. Lawrence), 3 Fiduc. Rep. 3d 10, annot. *Fiduc. Rev.*, Feb. 2013, p. 1.

Mother signed power of attorney naming son (one of her three children) as agent in May 2010. In February 2011, son engaged law firm to prepare irrevocable trust, which he signed both as trustee named therein and as Agent under his mother's power of attorney. Trust gave mother no rights in principal, but allowed principal distribution to be made to family members during her lifetime. After mother's complaint to Office of the Aging, which contended trust violated PEF Code provisions, assets were transferred back to mother. After mother's death, son filed a ". . . petition to restore the trust . . ." which was denied. *Edler Est.* (O.C. Div. Lycoming), 4 Fiduc. Rep. 3d 113, annot. *Fiduc. Rev.*, May 2014, p. 1.

Amendments in 1999 to PEF 5601(e)(4), as to agent's duty to keep records as to 4 checks in issue did not apply to power of attorney executed prior thereto. However, agent had duty to justify claimed disbursements by more than his unsupported testimony. Orphans' Court erred in relying solely on the amendment in imposing surcharge. Motion for counsel fees and costs was timely. *Bechtel Est.* (Pa. Super.), 92 A.3d 833.

*See Fiduciary Review*, Aug. 2014, p. 1 for summary of provisions of Act 96 of 2014 which amends provisions of Chapter 56 of PEF Code, particularly 5603 which revises gifting authorizations.

Act 95 of 2014 includes revised forms of NOTICE and ACKNOWLEDGMENT, as well as some modifications of provisions for Powers of Attorney signed after December 31, 2014. See *Fiduc. Rev.*, Dec. 2014, p. 3.

Power of Attorney did not support agent's action in closing mother's POD account and making gifts of proceeds to himself and brother, and excluding sister. *Coury Estate* (O.C. Div. Carbon), 4 Fiduc. Rep. 3d 436.

Agent used New Jersey power of attorney to transfer assets to himself and his wife. Personal representative sought return of assets. Agent contended that the "gifts" were valid under New Jersey law.

HELD: The gifts were void. *Moscowitz Est.*, 2015 Pa. Super. 23 (2/4/15), annot. *Fiduc. Rev.*, April 2015, p. 3.

Agent convicted of numerous counts of theft (and sentenced to 30-60 months imprisonment) for abuse of power of attorney, as agent for 86 year old aunt, by stealing nearly $300,000. Agent transferred principal's funds to himself. Power authorized making "unlimited gifts" but was not "a license to steal"; it was subject to agent's use of the power for the principal's benefit. *Comm. v. Patton*, Pa. Super. (#1973 W.D.A. 2012, 1974 W.D.A. 2012), Sept 19, 2014 (Non-precedential decision).

Agent who changed annuity beneficiary to charities without consulting incapacitated principal and without knowledge of will containing no charitable gifts has no ability to undo such designation after principal's death. *Scutchall Est.* (O.C. Div. Franklin), 5 Fiduc. Rep. 3d 311.

# Chapter 17

# WILL CONTESTS

---

## § 17.1 INTRODUCTION

"Before the court is the petition of Elizabethtown College for discovery relating to decedent's prior wills. The College contends that near the end of her life, the decedent, Florence M. Fasick, promised the College a bequest of approximately 97% of her estate. However, upon her death, her will left only 10% of her estate to the College and left 50% of the estate to the son of one of the decedent's friends who served as the decedent's agent under a power of attorney. In light of the large disparity between the decedent's promised gift and what the College ultimately would receive under the will, the College is requesting the executor to provide copies of any prior wills executed by the decedent. Essentially, the College seeks to discover whether there is some basis for a will challenge because of undue influence." The court allowed limited discovery. *Fasick Est.* (O.C. Div. Cumb.), 3 Fiduc. Rep. 3d 89, annot. *Fiduc. Rev.*, Mar. 2013, p. 1.

Decedent's children sought to contest will by challenges to final account; appeal dismissed. Appeal from probate exclusive method to contest will. Orphans' Court also correct in awarding additional counsel fees for defending against the appeal. *Estate of Whitley* (Pa. Super.), 50 A.3d 203.

In will contest involving allegations of undue influence, discovery subpoena directed to attorney-scrivener to produce documents associated with estate planning for decedent permitted under testamentary exception. *Cohen Est.* (O.C. Div. Bucks), 3 Fiduc. Rep. 3d 145.

Pennsylvania exception, in will contests, to the attorney-client privilege, is not applicable to dispute involving change of life insurance beneficiary designations. *Collautt v. Zhang* (U.S.D.C. E.D. Pa.), Civ. Action 14-632, 12/11/14.

## § 17.2 PARTIES IN INTEREST

Widow appealed from probate of estranged husband's will which left entire estate to children. Divorce action was pending and grounds had been established. It was held: Widow, being precluded from inheriting under PEF 2106(a), has no standing. Appeal dismissed. *Beal Est.* (O.C. Div. Phila.), 5 Fiduc. Rep. 3d 247, annot. *Fiduc. Rev.*, Sept. 2015, p. 2.

## § 17.3 ROLE OF THE PERSONAL REPRESENTATIVE

Appointment of administrator pro tem not warranted where no conflict on part of executrix; executrix found to have standing to defend the will but those benefitted may be liable for fee and costs. *Blusius Est.* (O.C. Div. Franklin), 4 Fiduc. Rep. 3d 207.

## § 17.4 GROUNDS FOR WILL CONTESTS

(1) Appeal from probate; will upheld against alleged lack of capacity and undue influence. Contestants' only evidence of incapacity was that decedent rambled at times and got off the track in conversation. *Cavanaugh Will* (O.C. Div. Monroe), 2 Fiduc. Rep. 3d 488.

Appeal from probate of 1988 will by proponents of 2001 will sustained where contestant of 2001 will failed to prove lack of capacity and failed to shift burden of proof re undue influence: *Lista Will* (O.C. Div. Phila.), 3 Fiduc. Rep. 3d 275.

(2) Decedent Kathryn Ehrhardt died September 6, 2009. The Register of Wills admitted to probate a writing of August 31, 2009 and granted letters to decedent's sister Zuzan. On November 12, 2009 decedent's only child Thomas filed an appeal from probate alleging lack of capacity and undue influence. Upon finding lack of testamentary capacity and finding undue influence based on confidential relationship, substantial benefit, and weakened intellect, Judge Linda Wallach Miller sustained the appeal and set aside the probate and grant of letters. *Ehrhardt Will* (O.C. Div. Monroe), 2 Fiduc. Rep. 3d 412, annot. *Fiduc. Rev.*, Oct. 2012, p. 3.

Contest based on alleged undue influence dismissed for failure to prove weakened intellect; late filed motion to amend appeal petition to raise issue of "suspicious circumstances" denied. *Cremers Will* (O.C. Div. Chester), 3 Fiduc. Rep. 3d 152.

Testator possessed testamentary capacity, but will was procured by undue influence. Pa. O.C. Rule 7.1 requires exceptions be filed to preserve issues on appeal if they were not preserved by objection, before trial court, but where they were raised in Rule 1925(b) statement that successfully preserved them. *Smaling Est.* (Pa. Super.), 80 A.3d 485.

Sheila's will of August 2011 was probated after Register dismissed caveat, and contestants (children and grandchildren) appealed, alleging fraud, undue influence, confidential relationship and forgery.

HELD: After extensive discovery, estate's motion for summary judgment granted. *Sayer Est.* (O.C. Div. Del.), 4 Fiduc. Rep. 3d 63, annot. *Fiduc. Rev.*, May 2014, p. 3.

Will was valid. Beneficiary did not exert undue influence; confusion and forgetfulness of testator at times prior to execution of will did not override evidence of lucidity around date of execution; impressions of scrivener and others as to condition of testator on date of execution are more probative of capacity than those of persons relying solely on review of medical records. *Nalaschi Est.* (Pa. Super.), 90 A.3d 8.

Five wills, executed between 1999 and 2011, all gave majority of estate to charities. A sixth will dated August 18, 2011 prepared by an attorney introduced to testatrix by her niece (who was also agent under her power of attorney) gave most of estate in trust for the niece. A later (final) will, prepared by scrivener of the prior wills, reverted to charitable dispositions.

HELD: Probate of last will upheld. *Flatlow Est.* (O.C. Div. Delaware), 5 Fiduc. Rep. 3d 69, annot. *Fiduc. Rev.*, June 2015, p. 3.

(3) "Petition to Strike Codicil" was filed, alleging invalidity because a subscribing witness was a minor, and a date had been inserted by counsel on the undated writing.

HELD: Petition dismissed, *Weitz Est.* (O.C. Div. Luzerne), 5 Fiduc. Rep. 3d., annot. *Fiduc. Rev.*, Jan. 2015, p. 4. Aff'd Pa. Super., #913 MDA 2014, 4/11/14.

(4) Petition to assess counsel fees and costs against the attorney did not prevail in trust litigation. Objections to trustee's account raised the issue as to whether the last amendment to the trust was forged. In finding against the objector, Judge Ott, of the Montgomery County Orphans' Court, said "The objectant's testimony was self-contradicting. Without the testimony of a handwriting expert or even of disinterested third parties familiar with the settlor's signature, there could be no basis for finding a forgery." *Keslar Trust* (O.C. Div. Montg.), 3 Fiduc. Rep. 3d 59, annot. *Fiduc. Rev.*, Feb. 2013, p. 4.

Master concluded that caveators' evidence that 2006 wills were forged was insufficient to prove forgery where there was extrinsic expert opinion evidence on both sides. *Karoly Est. and Angstadt Est.* (O.C. Div. Northampton), 2 Fiduc. Rep. 8d 452.

Sheila's will of August 2011 was probated after Register dismissed caveat, and contestants (children and grandchildren) appealed, alleging fraud, undue influence, confidential relationship and forgery.

HELD: After extensive discovery, estate's motion for summary judgment granted. *Sayer Est.* (O.C. Div. Del.), 4 Fiduc. Rep. 3d 63, annot. *Fiduc. Rev.*, May 2014, p. 3.

## § 17.7 TRIALS IN ORPHANS' COURT

(5) Order denying petition for removal of executrix is appealable under the collateral order doctrine. *Estate of Mumma*, 41 A.3d 41, 43 (n. 1).

# Appendix 4

# POST-DEATH TAX PLANNING CHECK LIST

**Affecting Income Taxes:**

9. *Pennsylvania inheritance tax discount.* Since the inheritance tax is now a deduction for federal estate tax purposes rather than a credit, even though the federal estate tax rate is 40 per cent for taxable estates, it is desirable to take advantage of the discount.

# Appendix 7

# SHORT-CUTS—STATUTORY PROVISIONS—PROTECTION OF FIDUCIARIES

**Decedent's Estates:**

Payments of deposit accounts *shall* be made to family up to $10,000 and payments from deceased patient's care account up to $10,000 may be made to funeral director: Act 35 of 2013.

Personal property distributed under court order is increased to $50,000: Act 35 of 2013.

# Appendix 12A

# FORM OF NOTICE TO DEPARTMENT OF PUBLIC WELFARE RE MEDICAL ASSISTANCE PAYMENTS

## ESTATE STATEMENT OF CLAIM REQUEST

**DECEDENT'S INFORMATION:**

| | |
|---|---|
| DECEDENT'S FULL NAME: | |
| LAST KNOWN COMPLETE ADDRESS: | |
| CITY, STATE, ZIP CODE: | |
| SOCIAL SECURITY NUMBER: | |
| DATE OF BIRTH: | |
| DATE OF DEATH: | |
| ESTIMATED VALUE OF DECEDENT'S ESTATE* (Please Include Written Documentation): | |

*If you know that the amount is either over or under $2,400, it is helpful if (at least) that is indicated.

**REPRESENTATIVE'S INFORMATION** ( EXECUTOR / ADMINISTRATOR / NEXT OF KIN ):

| | |
|---|---|
| REPRESENTATIVE'S NAME: | |
| RELATIONSHIP TO DECEDENT: | |
| P O BOX AND/OR STREET ADDRESS: | |
| CITY, STATE, ZIP CODE: | |
| DAYTIME PHONE NUMBER: | (     ) |

**ATTORNEY'S INFORMATION:**

| | |
|---|---|
| LAW FIRM NAME: | |
| ATTORNEY'S NAME: | |
| P O BOX AND/OR STREET ADDRESS: | |
| CITY, STATE, ZIP CODE: | |
| PHONE NUMBER: | (     ) |
| FAX NUMBER: | (     ) |

**SEND TO:**

**DEPARTMENT OF PUBLIC WELFARE**
**DIVISION OF THIRD PARTY LIABILITY**
**ESTATE RECOVERY PROGRAM**
P.O. BOX 8486
HARRISBURG, PA 17105-8486

**OR BY FACSIMILE:** (717) 772-6553 or (717) 705-8150

**ESTATE RECOVERY HOTLINE: 1-800-528-3708**
If you are calling from outside Pennsylvania, please call the Estate Recovery Program at (717) 772-6603